QUESTIONS OF BEING

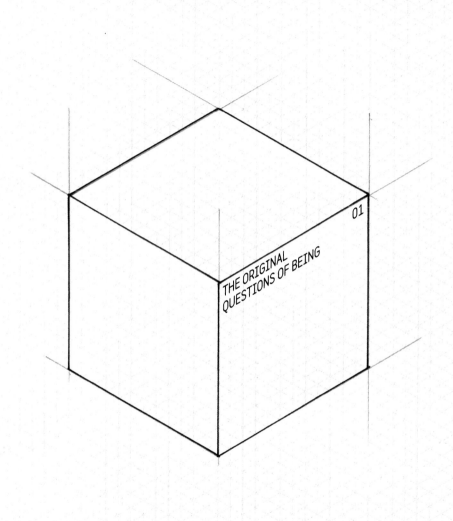

THE ORIGINAL
QUESTIONS OF BEING

01

SURE
WE CAN
BUILD PLANES
THAT FLY...

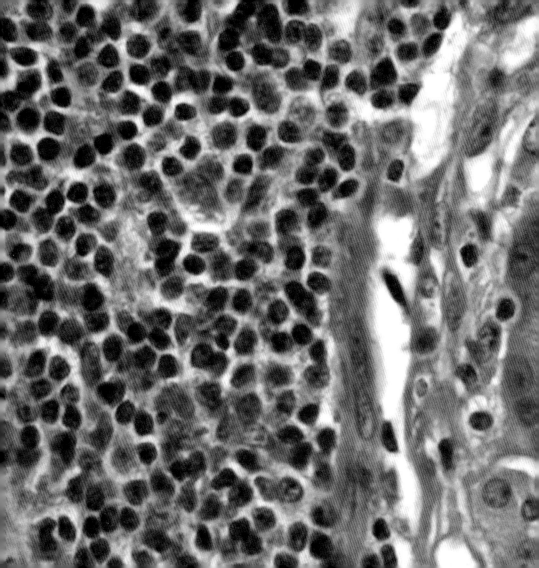

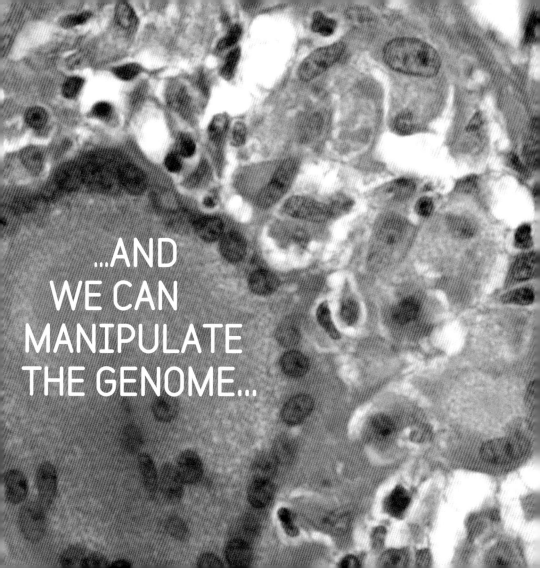

... BUT CAN WE ACTUALLY EXCEED THE 'LIMITS OF NATURE'?

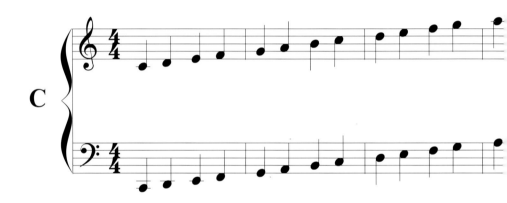

What would happen if everyone always did the right thing,

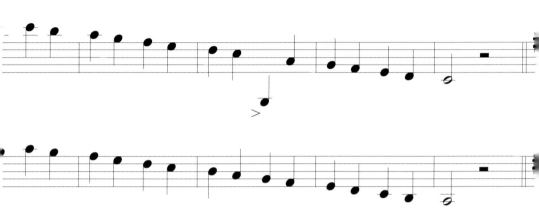

but then just one person didn't?

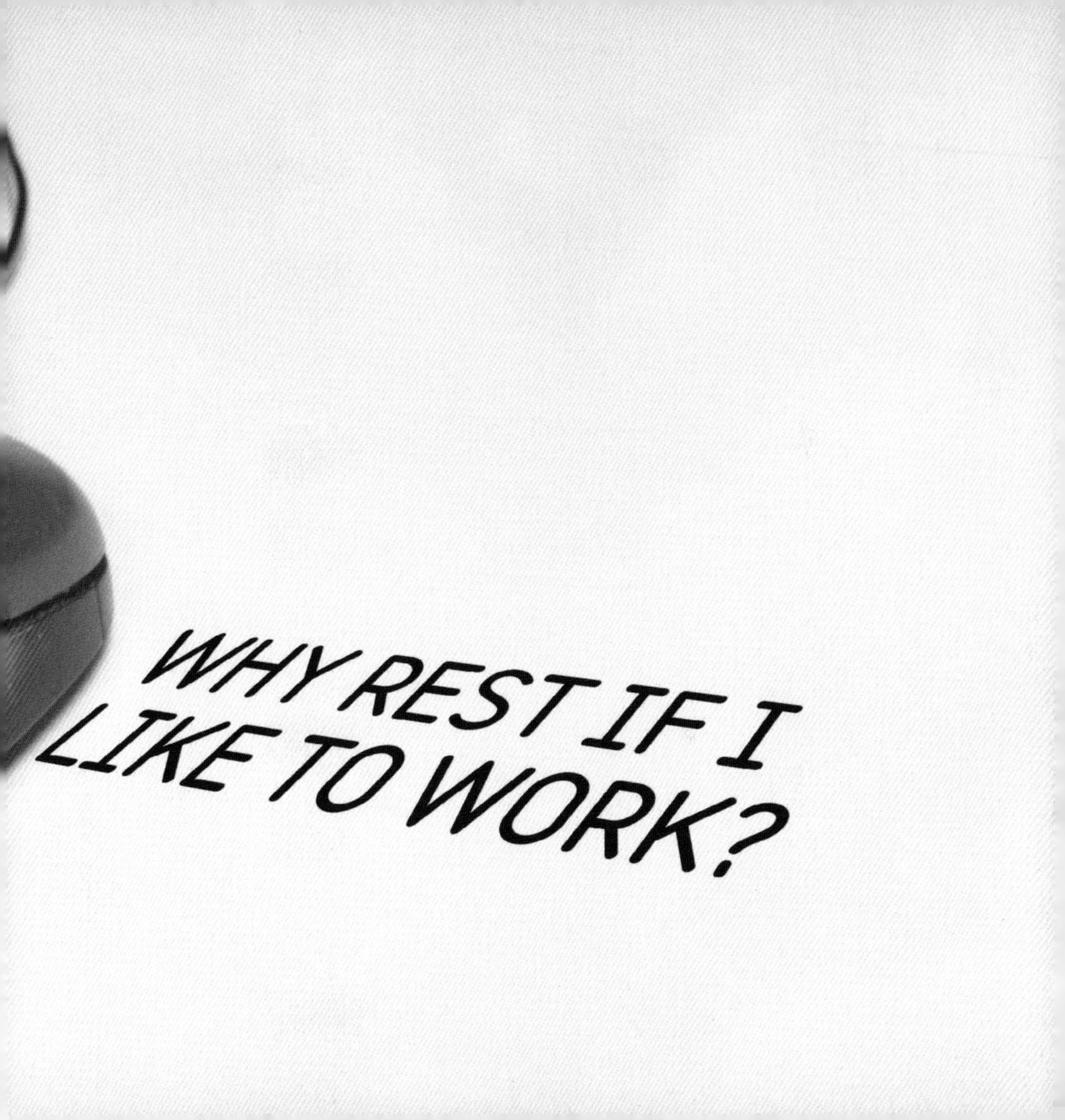
WHY REST IF I
LIKE TO WORK?

WHAT MAKES US SO INVENTIVE?

WHY DO WE STIFLE IT SO OFTEN?

PEOPLE
EAT AND SO DO
OTHER CREATURES.
NO ANIMAL HAS YET
OPENED A RESTAURANT.
HAS THAT EVER
STRUCK YOU AS
ODD?

qube

IF ALL
NATURE WAS
HUMMING
A TUNE,
WOULD
WE BE
LISTENING?

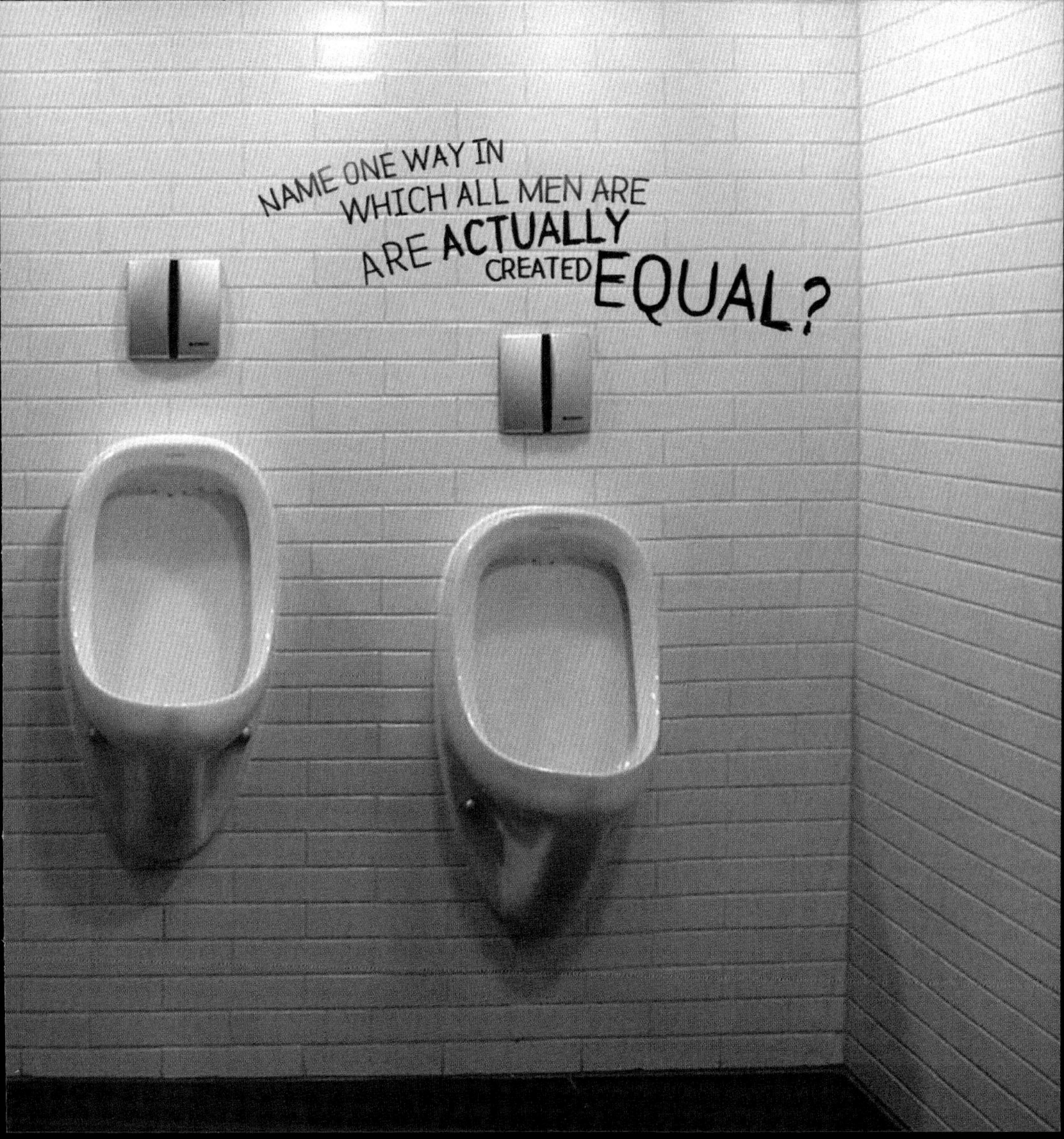
NAME ONE WAY IN
WHICH ALL MEN ARE
ARE ACTUALLY
CREATED EQUAL?

Children want
bedtime stories:

Why do they want their
stories to end happily?

Why are they unhappy
when the stories end?

fig 2.

fig 3.

THE AWKWARD
QUESTIONS OF BEING

02

You say,
'I haven't killed anyone'.

But if murder is considering
something that you want to be
of more value than the life of
another person;

...are you still so sure you haven't killed anyone?

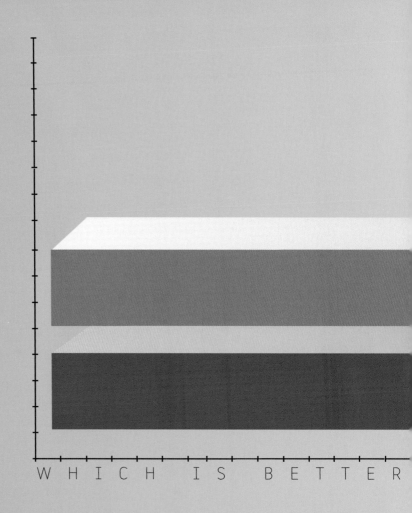

WHICH IS BETTER

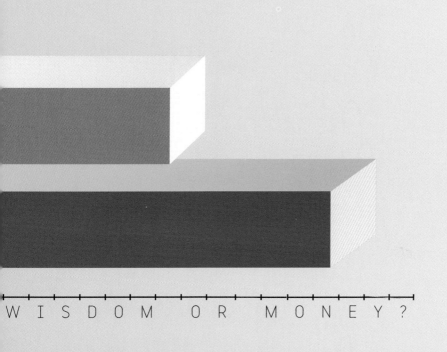

W I S D O M O R M O N E Y ?

Do you really believe
Do you really believe
Do you really believe
Do you really believe
Do you really believe
Do you really believ
Do you really belie
Do you really believ
Do you really beli
Do you really be

hat you say that you do?
what you say that you do?
what you say that you do?
what you say that you do?
what you say that you do?
what you say that you do?
what you say that you do?
what you say that you do?
what you say that you do?
what you say that you do?
ve what you say that you do?
eve what you say that you do
what you say that you d

COULD HISTORY BE OTHERWISE?

AND WHERE DO ALL THE UNFULFILLED POSSIBILITIES GO?

WHAT'S SO NATURAL ABOUT DYING?

(Just because everybody does something, doesn't make it natural.)

I
DO NOT
ALWAYS
DO WHAT I
KNOW IS RIGHT.

Is anything actually secure?

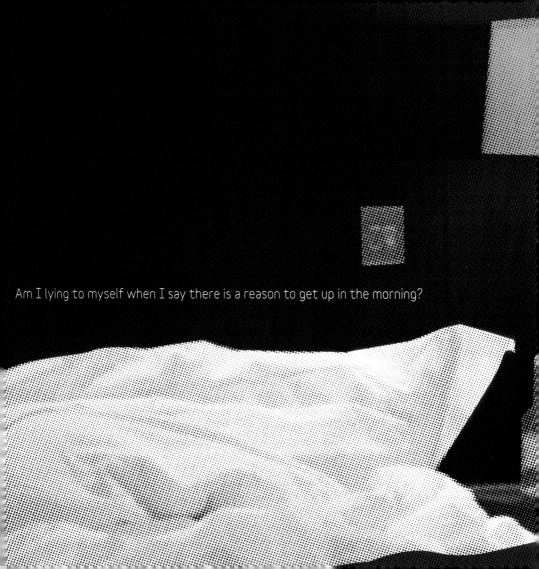

Am I lying to myself when I say there is a reason to get up in the morning?

THE RECOVERED
QUESTIONS OF BEING

03

To whom do you think you belong?

And who do you think belongs to you?

Before you say 'no-one'
realise that these answers are clues to your identity.

HOPE IS THE ABILITY TO IMAGINE A BETTER FUTURE.

A BETTER HOPE IS AN IMAGINED FUTURE

THAT TURNS OUT TO BE TRUE WHEN IT ARRIVES.

IS YOUR HOPE BETTER?

How can we continue to see with fresh eyes, peeled of their excuses?

I feel…. excited regret angry gla

EMOTIONS ARE SNEAKY THOUGHTS, BASED ON THE STORY WE TELL OURSELVES IS TRUE.

lonely guilty accepted encouraged pride reject

Taking your child and leaving them at an airport to go on without you is one of life's most profound experiences.

1

RECEIVED DAMAGED

- ☐ Handle broken
- ☐ Strap broken
- ☐ Scratch   ☐ Dent

SIDE

WHAT MAKES FOR GOOD SEX? IS IT MORE THAN JUST FRICTION?

I KNOW WHEN THINGS ARE WORKING
- EVEN THOUGH I DO NOT ALWAYS
KNOW HOW OR WHY.

HOPE IS THE ABILITY TO IMAGINE A BETTER FUTURE,
BUT I CANNOT PLACE MY HOPE IN ANYTHING THAT I KNOW IS IMAGINARY.

WE DO NOT ACTUALLY KNOW WHAT IS GOING TO HAPPEN NEXT -

THOUGH WE OFTEN CLAIM THAT WE DO.

WE FREQUENTLY KNOW WHAT IS GOING TO HAPPEN NEXT -

THOUGH WE CLAIM WE DO NOT.

YES OF COURSE,
BUT
WHY
IS THE GRASS ALWAYS GREENER
ON THE OTHER SIDE?

I AM NOT AT
HOME IN THE
ONLY WORLD
I HAVE EVER
KNOWN.

OK!

FIRST FOR CELEBRITY NEWS

ISSUE 113 • JUNE 5 1998 • £1.45 WEEKLY

"He told me he loved me..."

HUNKS OVER

DOES SOMETHING BECOME
MORE BEAUTIFUL, OR LESS,
WHEN WE UNDERSTAND IT?

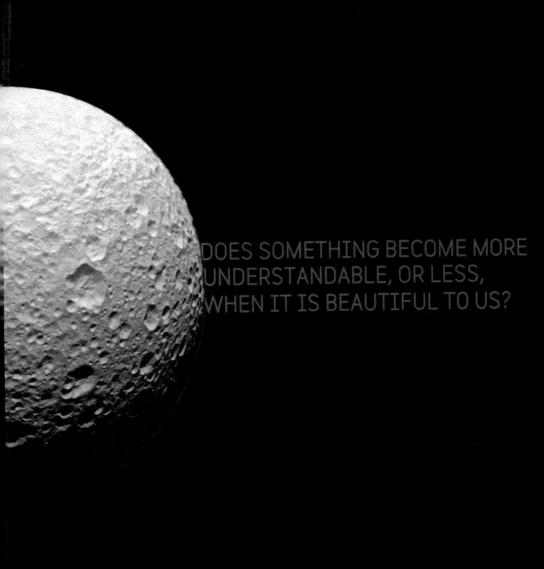

DOES SOMETHING BECOME MORE UNDERSTANDABLE, OR LESS, WHEN IT IS BEAUTIFUL TO US?

IS BEING GOOD A PATH OR A DESTINATION

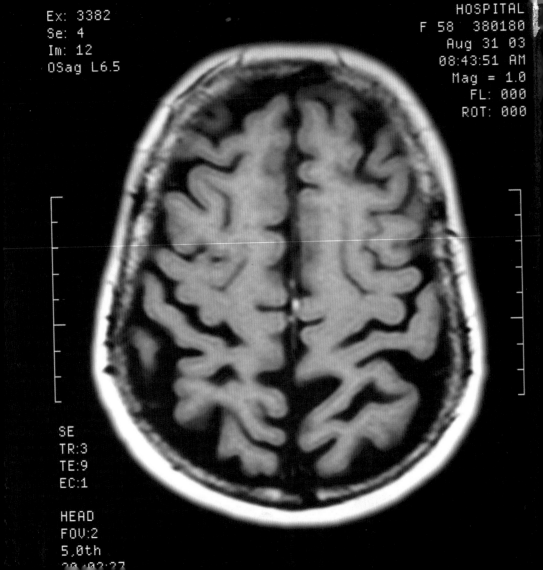

THE MORE I SEE, THE MORE I SEE THAT THERE IS MORE THAN I CAN SEE.

First Edition published 2008
By Pencil-Sharp Ltd

ISBN 978-0-9558836-0-6

Copyright © 2008, Pencil-Sharp Ltd

A CIP catalogue record for this book is available from the British Library.

Every care has been taken that all information was correct at the time of
going to press. The publishers accept no responsibility for any error in detail,
inaccuracy or judgement whatsoever.

Publishing Project Management by Pencil-Sharp Ltd
Designed and typeset by Sparks
Qube Books is an imprint of Pencil-Sharp Ltd
Printed and bound in the United Arab Emirates by Oriental Press Ltd